MW01232166

Mood

Swings

Mood

Swings

ASA Publishing Corporation
1285 N. Telegraph Rd., #376, Monroe, Michigan 48162
An Accredited Publishing House with the BBB
www.asapublishingcorporation.com

Copyrights©2020 Queen P, All Rights Reserved
Book Title: Mood Swings
Date Published: 09.02.2020 / Edition 1 *Trade Paperback*
Book ID: ASAPCID2380813
ISBN: 978-1-946746-81-8
Library of Congress Cataloging-in-Publication Data

This book was published in the United States of America.
Great State of Michigan

Table of Contents

Acknowledgments.. 1

Introduction.. 3

Dedication... 5

About the Poet..61

CHAPTER 1 - Discovery...11

Haiku #1 Prove It...12

Creating an Empire 13

Discover the Present 14

Pilgrimage..15

Your Purpose 16

Move Forward..17

CHAPTER 2 – Topsy Turvy 19

Haiku #2 Find Your Peace...20

Flashback 21

Redemption..22

You already Know 23

Betrayal..24

A True Friend 25

Gone Ghost..26

I'm in this Race..27

CHAPTER 3 – Lost in Emotion......................................29

Haiku #3 Reaching......................................30

Where did all the love go? 31

Private Love Affair......................................32

Don't know what to say 33

Where are you? 34

No Self-Control......................................35

Twilight Zone......................................36

CHAPTER 4 – Comfort 37

Haiku #4 That Feel Good Moment 38

Who Knew......................................39

Long Distance Love Affair......................................40

Morning Vibes......................................41

Comfort Space......................................42

It'll be just fine......................................43

Fantasy Place 44

CHAPTER 5 – This is Me 45

Haiku #5 I Am......................................46

Unapologetically Me......................................47

It's Complicated 48

Reflections......................................49

Relax 50

MOOD SWINGS

Note to Self 55

Acknowledgments

I give gratitude to the Almighty One for instilling in me the ability to express myself through writing poetry. I am in you, and you are in me. I am so grateful for this gift and elated beyond measure.

A huge appreciation to ASA Publishing Corporation for accepting and welcoming me into the ASA family. "It's been a fantastic journey this far, and I look forward to what lies ahead."

Then there's Mr. Mosley, "From day one, I knew that you were a unique soul with wisdom well beyond your years. Throughout my travels, you have opened my eyes and awakened me to a whole new world outside of the traditional realm. Thank you, Mr. Mosley, from the bottom of my heart for your inspiration and guidance towards my evolution."

As always, much love to my friends and family for your love and continued support. "You have no idea just how much you all mean to me." I am truly blessed.

Peace and Love
Queen P.

Queen P.

Introduction

We go through so many ups and downs in our lives. We experience joy, pain, happiness, sorrow and a plethora of emotions which sets the tone for our mood. It's amazing how your mood can change in a matter of minutes depending on what you're going through at that particular moment.

"When The Mood Is Right A Poetry Journey" took us on a spiritual journey. It allowed us to search our Soul, and find out who we are and what we want out of our lives.
"Mood Swings", part two of this trilogy, will reveal the moods that we encounter throughout our life's journey.

Without hesitation, we speak our mind. We're confident with who we are and are not afraid to speak our truth.

"Mood Swings" is going to take you to places inside and outside of yourself, and in the end, you'll find that whatever mood that's being experienced at that present time, is necessary for that particular moment.

No one is perfect, we all have mood swings; it's how we handle ourselves while we're going through it.

Are you ready to look at yourself for who you really are? Your truth shall set you free.

Are you ready?
Let's go!

Queen P.

*This book is dedicated
to everyone that's in a mood.*

Queen P.

"Take that mask off

Find a quiet place

To release the tension

And prepare to embrace"

Queen P.

Queen P.

THE JOURNEY CONTINUES . . . . . .

Queen P.

Chapter 1 - Discovery

Haiku #1
PROVE IT

Don't prove it to me

I already know what's true

Prove it to yourself

CREATING AN EMPIRE

First and foremost I am the Queen of this castle

With you my King there will be no more hassles

Building an empire is what we must plan

With you beside me, united we stand

From the bottom to the top, we'll work our way up

Unleashing our power there will be no division

Creating a legacy that defines our vision

Flying high with great expectations

The Queen has spoken without hesitation

This is our season of manifestation

DISCOVER THE PRESENT

I can tell you all about the past but
I cannot predict the future.
Learned quite a bit from what we endured and know
that we have thoroughly matured.

Resurrecting our minds, detangling all the confusion.
Planning ahead, searching for a reason.

Come walk with me, come take my hand, let's discover
what's in the present. Together, I can guarantee what we
find will be well worth it.

PILGRIMAGE

You see I'm on this pilgrimage

Ready to unwind myself

Going to define myself

Looking to rewind myself

Not to undermine myself

Hoping to refine myself

Having quality time with myself

Not going to deny myself

You see I'm on this pilgrimage

In search of....

YOUR PURPOSE

Do you know your purpose
Are you asking why
Can you comprehend your existence
Are you willing to give it a try

Take that mask off
Find a quiet place
To release the tension
And prepare to embrace

The moment of truth
Getting deeper into your inner self
Meditating on the gifts that were given to you

Anxious at the thought of what is yet to come
Fear of the unknown yet wanting to know more

Your presence is a gift and very much desired
Dive in and get to know yourself
For your action is required

MOVE FORWARD

Oh, so innocent ever so naive

Living that sheltered life not knowing what to believe

Running to the left, shuffling to the right

Like a puppet on a string with no direction in sight

Keep searching, move forward, your destination is near

Unveil the knowledge so your own pathway will be clear.

Queen P.

Chapter 2 - Topsy Turvy

Haiku #2

FIND YOUR PEACE

Chaos has ensued

Frequencies have gone awry

Needing to recharge

FLASHBACK

Flashing back memories of the way it used to be.

Thankful for the experiences, bringing me through adversity.

Reminiscing about past loves that once were, but realizing now they were

Only for a season.

Aware that they came into my life for a reason.

Lessons of life, lessons learned.

Nothing ventured, nothing gained.

Moving on to a higher plane.

Understanding that those days are over,

No more looking over my shoulders.

My past generated the changes in me,

Now I'm prepared to seek what's best for me.

Flashing back memories of the way it used to be,

Never forgetting that part of my history.

REDEMPTION

Pacing back and forth,
Plagued by my own decisions.
Wondering how to make things right,
Not going to give up the fight.

Why is this such a production?
Losing you was not an option.
I considered you to be my main attraction.
You once always gave me protection.

Simply waiting for a reaction.
Seems as if you've become a distraction.
No more pacing back and forth.
Listening to that inner voice.
Letting me know the battle is over.
No more going under cover.

Shaking off the pain and sorrow.
Building up the strength for tomorrow.
Thank you for this interruption.
Redeeming myself, I have recovered.

YOU ALREADY KNOW

Stay on course and ignore the distractions.

Listen to yourself because you know just what you need.

That gut instinct will give you the answers.

Momentary distractions steer you away from your truth.

Take a moment, dig deep into your soul

and receive the message

'Cause you already know.

BETRAYAL

So many broken promises and lies that have been told.

Excluding me from all discussions, keeping me out in the cold.
You having the upper hand and taking full command,

has put me in a headspace searching to find self-control.

See I was birthed by a Queen, raised to be treated with respect;

Therefore, we need to have a conversation to put things back in check.

Let's go back to being equals, we should give it one more try.

If we fall short with our intentions, then we must finally say goodbye.

A TRUE FRIEND

Warm-hearted, gentle and kind, always giving and forgiving. The one you can trust and call on when you're in a bind, always lending a hand and never judging. A ride or die friend forever.

Now the tables have turned and the same attention is needed, yet not equipped to reciprocate the same gestures.

Am I out of my mind? Am I overthinking? I thought I knew the meaning of true friendship.

Mutual feelings? No! I understand, because what you are to me is just an acquaintance.

GONE GHOST

I believed in you, I trusted you
I would do anything for you.
You turned my gray skies into blue.
I want to know what happened to you?

You have fallen far from grace
Leaving without even one trace,
Reckless behavior without hesitation
Denying me an explanation.

Show a little decency
Come back to explain why you did this to me.

Needing to get my life back in order
All that's left now, is having some closure.

MOOD

I'M IN THIS RACE

Chasing after my dreams

I'm ready to soar

It's time to be seen

I'm ready to roar

My voice is loud and strong

Been quiet for too long

Coming out from behind the shadows

Finding my way through the clouds

Unveiling myself to show my face

No longer a benchwarmer

I'm in this race

Queen P.

Chapter 3 - Lost in Emotion

Haiku #3

REACHING

My eyes tightly closed

Creating visions of you

Reaching for your soul

WHERE DID ALL THE LOVE GO?

Where did all the love go

Why is there so much pain

Fools in love won't last forever

Barely having it all together

Vulnerable ones finding each other

Searching for love in one another

So weak and immature

Desires of the heart for love to implore

Where did all the love go

Why is there so much pain

Taking it all in stride

While thoughts of you still remain

PRIVATE LOVE AFFAIR

I want to love you

I don't know how to tell you

Private love affair

DON'T KNOW WHAT TO SAY

There are so many things that I meant to say but I just
forgot to tell you.

There were so many things that I wanted to say while
standing right beside you.

What is this spell that you have on me?

Having me lose my memory,

Subconscious mind in the galaxies,

Not knowing what is reality.

There are so many things that I want to say, but you keep
on doing this to me.

WHERE ARE YOU?

I see you in my dreams.

The sound of your voice is in my head.

Your presence is all around me.

Where are you?

NO SELF-CONTROL

Working hard to get the job done.
The blinders are on, distracted by no one.

Having it all together, the focus is clear,
The goals are set, I'm almost there.

Suddenly I look up and in front of me is
the only one who can distract me.

To make me lose my concentration,
To whisk me away from all of my troubles.

"Surprise! He says, I just had to see you,
You were on my mind and I really need you."

Tempted to fall right into his arms but if I do,
It will cause great harm.

Must finish the work but he needs my attention.
What do I do now? Why all this confusion?

He traveled so far just to see me
I cannot ignore him, I know that he needs me.

The love of my life, my one true love.
He'll understand and wait 'till I'm done.

Must stay focused and finish this one
Who am I kidding, baby here I come.

NO SELF-CONTROL

THE TWILIGHT ZONE

So gentle and so kind
The heart flutters when you enter my mind
Love me like you did before
My body is numb, I drop to the floor

Slowly exploring as if it were the first time
Lost in the universe, galaxies far away
Beating hearts at a steady pace
This moment can never be erased

I think I'm in the twilight zone
Back in time
Not wanting to go home

Chapter 4 - Comfort

Haiku #4
THAT FEEL GOOD MOMENT

Lying here in bed

Thoughts of you come rushing through

Instantly I smile

WHO KNEW

I thought I was in love

I thought I knew how to love

Then you came along

and changed the definition

LONG DISTANCE LOVE AFFAIR

No need to worry, no need to fear. We're in this together, we'll always be near.

At times it may seem as if there's no way around, this long distance love affair,

It seems so profound.

I feel you whenever, wherever I go, the smile on my face just brings out this glow.

At times it may seem as if there's no way around, this long distance love affair,

It seems so profound.

Oh boy, your energy surrounds me, there's no one else around me

Oh yeah, it's a bond that can't be broken even when words are unspoken.

Oh boy, you bring me joy!

At times it may seem as if there's no way around, this long distance love

affair, it seems so profound.

MORNING VIBES

Woke up this morning

Joyful

That morning stretch

Elation

The sound of silence

Meditation

Embracing today without

Hesitation

COMFORT SPACE

Sitting by the fireplace,
Cozy, comfortable and warm.

Listening to the crackle and pop,
With the aroma of Cedar flowing.

The room is ablaze with light
on this cold, windy, wintry night.

Eyes heavy, slowly drifting away
to another place.

Physically present, the mind wandering
off into outer space.

IT'LL BE JUST FINE

That special place, that private space

A time to erase, to be displaced

For a moment in time, to merely unwind

To clear the mind

It will be just fine

FANTASY PLACE

Take me to a place that nobody knows
Where not everyone goes
Criticism free and no judgment at all
Where we stand united with justice for all

Find me that place where I look at you and you
look at me and we nod and smile graciously
There's no fear of you and no fear of me
We're equal in totality

Find me that place where true words are spoken
no lies or deceit
where no one is broken

Take me there, I'll go in haste
Take me to that enchanted place.

Chapter 5 - This Is Me

Haiku #5
I AM

I am who I am

Your words do not define me

I control my life

UNAPOLOGETICALLY ME

They say that I'm a mystery that they don't understand.

How I'd rather spend time with myself than to join in with the gang.

But why should assimilate? I can only be, the unique woman that I am

Unapologetically.

IT'S COMPLICATED

They ask me why I'm so quiet, they say Is something
wrong?
I say that everything's alright just listening to this song.

So let me have this moment, just let me have my space to
take in
all the sentiments that have me in this special place.

I may burst into laughter, I might burst into tears, worry
not my dear
friend, I'm reflecting through the years.

At times I loved with no connection and times I loved
with high vibrations.
Right now I'm in my quiet place, a time that cannot be
traded.
I hope that you can understand, I know it's complicated.

REFLECTIONS

Lying here reflecting on some moments of the past. Words that were embedded in my head to make me feel less than.

"You'll never get too far in life because you are not smart enough, because your house is not big enough and where you live, the area is too rough.

The clothes that you wear are not expensive enough. You really just don't fit in, you're way too different from the rest of us,"

I'm so grateful for all of the negativity that's been thrown at me, I used it all as ammunition to create my own reality.

The house, the clothes, and all of the non-essentials is where I want them to be.

I'm different and I don't fit in 'cause that's how I want it

to be. As for my dark chocolate Brown skin, my definition,

It's more than enough.

One more thing, my kinky hair, hands off, PLEASE DO NOT TOUCH!

RELAX

Time to relax your mind and leave your worries behind,
no one ever said that life was fair. It's a struggle yes,
But you will get there.

Don't worry 'bout what people say, it's not their life, you
live your life your own way. Get to know you and learn to
love yourself, then put your drama on the bottom shelf.

It's time to wake up and set yourself free from all of the
hatred and misery. So just relax and ease your mind and
leave all your worries behind, No one ever said that life
would be fair, it's a struggle yes, but your peace is near.

"I sing because I'm happy,
I sing because I'm free,
For his eye is on the sparrow,
And I know He watches me."

Civilla D. Martin
Charles H. Gabriel

Queen P.

EMBRACE THE MOMENT

Queen P.

MOOD SWINGS: Note to Self

I put together a few questions that you might want to ask yourself as you continue on your journey. Take the next couple of pages to deeply explore your Mood Swings.

1. Do you know where you're going and are you on the right track?

2. What methods are you using for finding your peace?

3. How does being in love affect you during challenging moments?

4. What do you do or where do you go to find comfort?

5. Who are you?

6. Are you being true to yourself?

MY MOOD SWINGS

MY MOOD SWINGS

MY MOOD SWINGS

MY MOOD SWINGS

IT'S NOT OVER ....

About the Author & Poet

Queen P was born in Manhattan, NY. She is the youngest of 4 children. Queen P graduated from NYIT (New York Institute of Technology) with a BFA in Communication Arts. She has worked in the entertainment industry all of her adult life but finds poetry to be her desired passion. With her first book "When The Mood Is Right: A Poetry Journey" under her belt, she desires to continue to pursue her passion of writing poetry in hopes that it will uplift and bring a breath of life to someone traveling on that road to infinity.

Made in the USA
Las Vegas, NV
13 November 2020

10756435R00046